MW00659074

Soul
of
Japan

Photography by **Katsuhiko Mizuno**
and **Hidehiko Mizuno**
Text by **Yoji Yamakuse**

Soul
of
Japan

The Visible Essence

Soul of Japan

The Visible Essence

Annotated Photographs
to Explain the Essence of Japanese Thought

奉

IBC Publishing

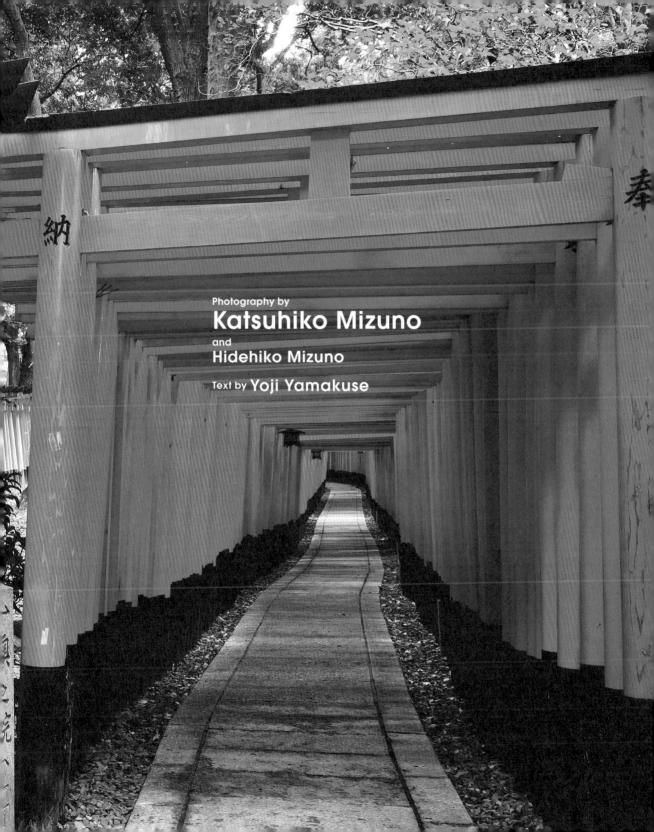

Photography by
Katsuhiko Mizuno
and
Hidehiko Mizuno

Text by **Yoji Yamakuse**

Photographs by Katsuhiko Mizuno and Hidehiko Mizuno
except page 32 by Amana images
Text by Yoji Yamakuse
Translation by Michael A. Cooney
Design by KEI SAITO
DTP by Hiromi Hishiki

Decorative full-page endsheets from *Shikosha Design Library*
used courtesy of Stone Bridge Press

Published by IBC Publishing, Inc.
Ryoshu Kagurazaka Bldg. 9F, 29-3 Nakazato-cho
Shinjuku-ku, Tokyo 162-0804
www.ibcpub.co.jp

First Edition 2012

ISBN 978-4-7946-0135-3
Printed in Japan

Contents

Preface

Many people, in days gone by, have made innumerable attempts to enlighten the West about traditional Japanese thought and the country's system of values—that is, "the heart of Japan."

This effort started in the distant past with Inazo Nitobe's *Bushido: The Soul of Japan* and Tenshin Okakura's *Book of Tea*, and in the postwar period it continued with the publication of countless similar works.

And not to be forgotten is the well-known book by Ruth Benedict that was begun near the end of World War II and finished after the war—*The Chrysanthemum and the Sword*.

One thing that is shared by all these works is their emphasis on "obligation" and "duty" as central principles in the Japanese value system. Where did these values come from, and what place do they have in modern Japanese life? In an attempt to answer this daunting question, I examine in this book 50 aspects of the "Japanese heart."

When Japanese people speak in English about Japanese thought processes and value systems, there is one thing they should definitely avoid: treating Japan as a special case. All countries and cultures have something unique in their value systems, and the Japanese value system is nothing but one particular example. There is also the fact that Japan has had a nuanced relationship

with certain Asian value systems, and quite a few of their values have found nourishment in Japanese soil and become deeply embedded in the Japanese psyche. It is important, I think, to make an objective view of Japanese values more widely available, and at the same time to remove the need for "excuses" when Japanese individuals find it hard to give a clear-cut description of Japanese values to foreigners.

In the present book I have paid particular attention to the connections between different values. Furthermore, in order to make it easier to explain the Japanese mental world to foreigners, a photograph accompanies each of the concepts as a visual aid.

Some of the values that might appear antiquated today are still lingering in the further recesses of the minds of modern Japanese, having changed their forms but retained their influence. Other values may generate behavior that leads to potential misunderstandings with non-Japanese people. In such ways as this, I have examined Japanese values from various perspectives, hoping to pin them down.

I will be immensely pleased if, by reading this book, you can grasp the connections between the various elements of the Japanese heart, relating them to your own experiences and history.

Yoji Yamakuse

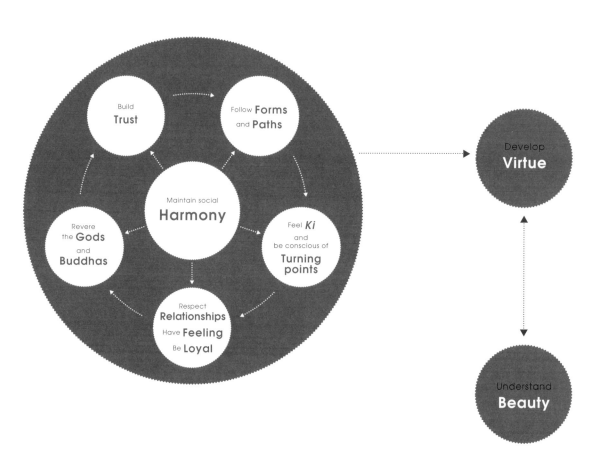

On Reading the Japanese Heart

If we take harmony (*wa*), the first value to be dealt with in this book, as the principal value in the Japanese system and position it in the center, showing its relative relation to other values, then we get the illustration seen below.

No matter what the culture, if its constituent values can coexist and function together without friction, the people inhabiting that culture feel a sense of tranquility.

Harmony represents tranquility for the Japanese, and in order to achieve it, a Japanese will adhere to the various values, norms, and moral precepts described in this book.

In Japan, a person who embodies the totality of values inherent in harmony is a person of virtue and can also embody the Japanese sense of beauty.

If you have reference to this illustration while reading the book, you will be able to understand how each value is linked to the others.

Soul
of
Japan

The Visible Essence

和を保つ

Maintain Harmony

Harmony (*wa*) is the harmonious heart
of the Japanese value system.

 Wa

Harmony

Japan's traditions evolved in the context of a collaborative agricultural society. People had to work together on a limited amount of land to raise the rice crop, so the needs of the group were given priority over those of the individual. Harmony or *wa* is about understanding and accommodating other people's point of view to ensure that the group can take action smoothly and effectively.

謙讓 謙遜 (Kenjō, Kenson)

Modesty

One way the Japanese achieve harmonious relationships is by putting egotism to one side. They never boast about their abilities or regard themselves as superior. The way Japanese parents introduce their children—"This is my good-for-nothing son"—is an example of this modesty in action. Paradoxically, being humble may send out a message that you actually have plenty to be proud of. Think of the old Japanese expression: "The heavier the stock of rice, the lower its head."

Ba

Place, Situation

In Japan it is important to behave in a situation-appropriate manner. A Japanese businessman, for example, will conduct himself differently at a formal meeting with a customer, a meeting with his boss and a night out with his colleagues. *Ba o wakimaeru* refers to the ability to sense what the proper behavior is in a given time and place. An ability to "read situations" and act accordingly is key to mastering Japanese etiquette.

Ma

Space

Ma means a space or interval in time or distance. In the feudal era, it was taboo for ordinary people to approach nobles. They had to speak to them from a distance and a lower position, or even through an intermediary. Space between people is the basis of the concept of ma.

Ma can also refer to time. For instance, if a difficult subject comes up in conversation, the Japanese might put it aside for a while and return to it later. The expression for this is sukoshi ma o oku, meaning to "take a little pause."

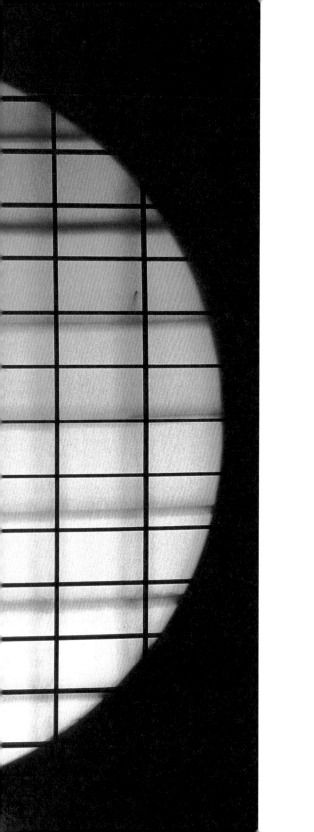

Chapter

2

型・道に従う

Follow Forms and Paths

Forms (*kata*) are the concrete
know-how by which a skill is learned.
A path (*michi*) is the spiritual value by which
a skill is strengthened.

型 Kata

Form

Kata is about following ceremonies and etiquette correctly. It is a form of behavior appropriate to a particular place and time. You can see *kata* at work in all aspects of Japanese life. The exchange of name cards, the pre-bout rituals of sumo, even the mundane act of pouring and receiving a cup of sake—these are all examples of *kata*.

Kata also influences the way the Japanese work. They do not like to proceed by trial and error; they prefer to master the *kata*—the best way to do a thing—before they start.

技 Waza

Skill

Repeated practice results in mastery of a skill, or *waza*. But even after mastering a *waza*, one must remain modest and further polish (*migaku*) one's skills. The idea of polishing one's skills comes from the samurai habit of assiduously polishing a sword to bring out its best.

Training someone in a *waza* is not just about imparting a single narrow skill. The teacher's goal is to make the student a more rounded person in every aspect of life.

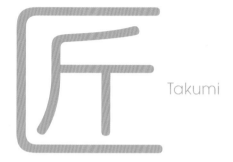

Takumi

Craft

In Japan people who are masters of traditional handicrafts are said to have *takumi* (craft). As more and more things are created through mass production, the Japanese are waking up to the special worth of products created by individual artisans whose skills have been honed over a lifetime. (Of course, there are parts of the mass-production process—things like polishing or grinding—that require the sort of intuition and precision that only a human with *takumi* can achieve). Accepting the traditional teacher-student relationship is an important part of passing *takumi* from one generation to the next.

Way

Just as in English, the Japanese word *michi* (also pronounced *dō*), meaning "path" or "way," is used as a metaphor for life's journey. A person living an immoral life will thus be described as *fudōtoku*, or "not on the road of virtue." *Michi* also refers to the spiritual values of a particular skill. *Kadō* (written with the characters for "flower" and "way") is the art of flower arrangement; *kendō* is the art of sword fighting; and *shintō* is the way of the gods, or the native religion of Japan.

Michi

武士道 Bushidō

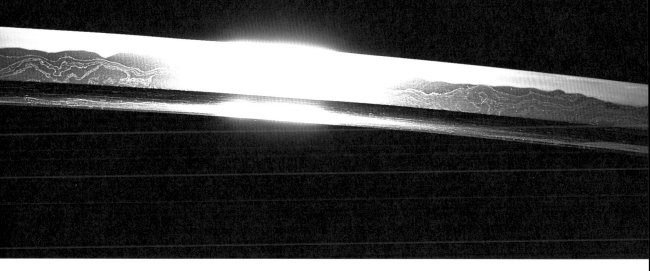

The Way of the Warrior

Bushi is another word for samurai, so *bushidō* means "the way of the warrior." Unquestioning loyalty to one's master, bravery in the face of danger, fearlessness of death, the mastery of desire and the willingness to live a simple life—these were the key values of the samurai. But these values did not die out in feudal times. Many Japanese businessmen now go about their jobs with a similar spirit of loyalty and self-sacrifice. Indeed, in 1899 philosopher and diplomat Inazo Nitobe wrote a book arguing that *bushidō* was Japan's answer to Christianity and the source of all moral law.

Seeking the Truth

Training and studying hard to reach a goal is called *gudō*. The Japanese set a high value on the sincerity of a person's efforts to accomplish something even if the results ultimately fall short. Regardless of the final outcome, they believe that just making the attempt can be a valuable learning experience with spiritual benefits.

Gudō

気を感じ、節を意識する

Feel *Ki*,
Be Aware of Transition

Ki describes the invisible movement of energy in our world.
Transition (*setsu*) is an important turning point in life.

気

Ki

Energy

Ki is a concept that originated in ancient China (where it is called *chi*) to describe the movement of unseen energy in our world. Walking in the clear morning air one feels refreshed. That is an example of positive *ki*. By contrast, the angry feelings generated by an argument are an example of negative *ki*. The Japanese admire people who are attuned to the *ki* (energy flow, atmosphere) of any given moment and adapt their behavior to accommodate others' needs.

Milestones

A *fushime* means an "important point of transition in life." To understand the concept, picture a piece of bamboo. A bamboo stalk is divided into *fushime* ("nodes") and growth from node to node results in the fully grown plant. So it is in life, where each specific period builds on the previous one. The idea of continuity is thus an important part of the concept of *fushime* and it explains why, when the Japanese complete something, they like to hold ceremonies and thank people, before moving on to the next stage.

 Setsu

Chapter

4

Have Feeling,
Be Loyal

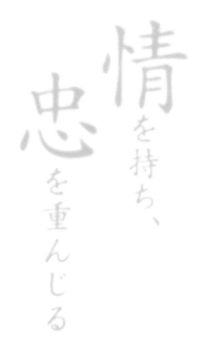

Feeling (*jō*) refers to emotions of all kinds:
happiness, sadness, pleasure, distress.
Loyalty (*chū*) means to respect and serve a person
from whom one has received a favor.

Feelings

Jō refers to feelings of all kinds: happiness, sadness, pleasure, distress. Westerners often criticize Japanese television dramas for being too sentimental. This is because the Japanese tend to express their emotions indirectly—for example,

Jō

through tears—rather than directly through words and gestures. *Jō* is all about expressing emotions nonverbally, and for the Japanese this is the most beautiful form of expression of all.

義理

Giri

Obligation, Duty

In Japanese ethics it is very important to be aware of, and to repay, one's obligations (*giri*) to others. The conflict between obligation and personal feeling (*ninjō*) is a popular theme in traditional performing arts like kabuki or *bunraku* puppet theater. A classic *giri-ninjō* theme might be a daughter who became engaged to one man to fulfill her duty toward her father, while her true affections were directed at another man. On a more everyday note, *giri* can also be seen in rituals like giving gifts or visiting clients at the year-end.

人情

Ninjō

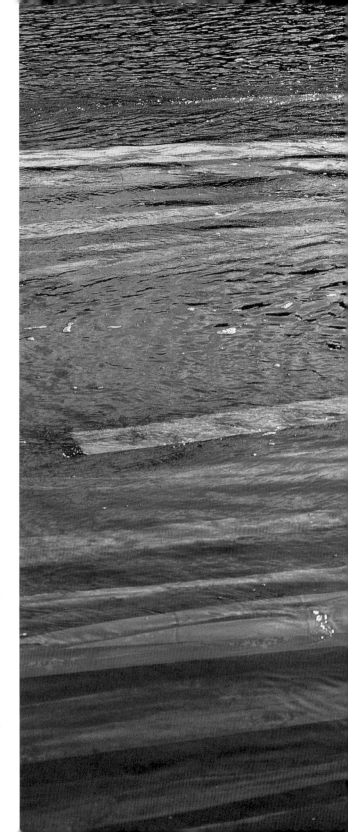

Personal Feelings

The Japanese are reluctant to accept the idea that "business is business." They do not want to exclude personal feelings (*ninjō*) from the professional sphere. To give an example, people would applaud a judge who gave a milder sentence to a criminal in consideration of the difficult environment he came from. Why? Because it would be an example of *ninjō*—sympathizing with the less fortunate—in action.

内
と
外

Uchi to Soto

Inside and Outside

The Japanese regard people to whom they are close as "inside" (*uchi*) and those with whom they have a more distant, impersonal relationship as "outside" (*soto*). To reduce the risk of emotional complications, the Japanese tend to be open about their personal feelings only with people they feel are inside their social circle. In the business world, the Japanese like to go out for dinner and drinks with their counterparts to build a relationship in which both parties can be "inside." This, they believe, will help business go better.

Loyalty

The concept of *chū* means respecting and serving a person (often of high rank) from whom one has received a favor. In feudal times, when rank and position were more clearly defined than today, *chū* was thus a more important ethical norm than it is now. It can still be seen in the loyalty Japanese people have for their companies, and their willingness to sacrifice themselves for the good of the group.

Chū

Kō

Filial Piety

Under the system of Confucian morals, children were expected to treat their parents—especially the father—with the utmost respect and consideration. During the feudal period, they even had to address them as if they were persons of a different rank. This attitude, called *kō* (filial piety), exists not just in Japan, but other Confucian countries like Korea. These days the relationship of parent and child is much more casual, but filial piety is still considered an important social value.

Revere the Gods
and Buddhas

Chapter

5

The unique spiritual values of Japan
were created by the native Shinto religion in combination
with elements of Buddhism from Asia.

神 Kami

The Gods

When Japanese refer to *kami*, they usually mean the gods of Shinto religion, the indigenous religion of Japan. In Shinto there are multiple gods who reside in waterfalls, rocks, lakes and large trees. As worshippers of the mysteries of nature, the Japanese liked to purify themselves before natural objects through ascetic training. Sitting beneath a mountain waterfall is an example of such a religious rite. The native Shinto religion later mixed with elements of Buddhism from Asia to create the unique spiritual values of Japan.

Purification

For the Japanese of old, it was important to mark the distinction between ordinary life and the time one spent in the presence of the gods by purifying oneself. That is why even now the Japanese wash their hands and rinse their mouths before entering a shrine to pray. The act of *misogi* can also be seen in people pouring watering over themselves at country festivals, jumping into the cold ocean on New Year's Day, or standing under waterfalls in the mountains. Such rituals are not just about cleaning the body—they also cleanse the soul.

Misogi 禊

Defilement

Kegare is a condition of pollution or defilement in the Shinto religion. Causes include contact with death, childbirth or disease. Children and virgin girls are naturally pure, but adults, inevitably, are not. They therefore have to go through purification rites at shrines or other places of worship to rid themselves of their *kegare* because they cannot present themselves to the gods in a polluted or defiled state.

Kegare

清廉

Seiren

Integrity

Confucian philosophy urges the putting aside of personal interest for the greater good of the public. *Seiren* is the virtue of having a pure heart with no selfish, personal ambitions. The phrase *seiren-keppaku* ("integrity and purity") refers to acting with absolute impartiality, avoiding all shame or dishonor.

The concept of *seiren* merged with the Buddhist values of Zen and samurai values of *bushidō* to produce a way of thinking that found beauty in simplicity. The ultimate expression of this is probably the minimalism of the Japanese rock garden.

Gan

Request

People pray for a variety of things at shrines: for a child to get into a good high school or university, for instance, or for the success of a business venture. This sort of request to the gods is called *gan*. When making such a request of the gods, the Japanese believe they should purify themselves and get their desires under control. By this token, a man who liked alcohol might stand a better chance of his prayers being answered if he gave up drinking for the duration.

 Butsu

Buddhism

Buddhism is thought to have reached Japan in the seventh century. In its early period, it was focused on Buddha the man, but gradually, as more sects developed, it became about a god who relieved human suffering. It also changed from a meditative discipline targeting enlightenment to one based on chanting in a quest for salvation in the next world. Unlike Shinto, Buddhism encourages a belief in the afterlife.

The Other World

In colloquial Japanese the afterlife is called *ano yo* ("the other world"). One stock character in Japanese ghost stories is the spirit who cannot cross to the other world because he remains bound to this one. For example, a person who has been murdered cannot go on to the other world until his killer has been executed or driven to suicide. Going to the other world is called *jōbutsu,* or becoming a Buddha, when one rids oneself of the bitterness and concerns of this world and enters paradise.

Ano Yo

もののの哀れ Mono no Aware

Pathos

Mono no aware is the sense of pathos the Japanese feel when contemplating the fleetingness of life. Cherry blossom viewing is an example of this sense of pathos in action. The blossoms give pleasure but also arouse feelings of pathos because their beauty will last only a few days. Japanese literature is full of examples of this aching appreciation of transient beauty from the Heian period onward. *Mono no aware* is a crucial component of the Japanese sense of beauty.

Transience

Things are constantly changing. Everything that lives will eventually die. All that is glorious is doomed to decay. Nothing can maintain its current form forever—such is the concept of *mujō*. The beginning of the famous epic song from the Middle Ages, *The Tale of the Heike*, states: "everything is ephemeral, nothing is constant." The story then goes on to show transience in action, depicting the decline of the powerful Heike family at the hands of their rivals.

Mujō

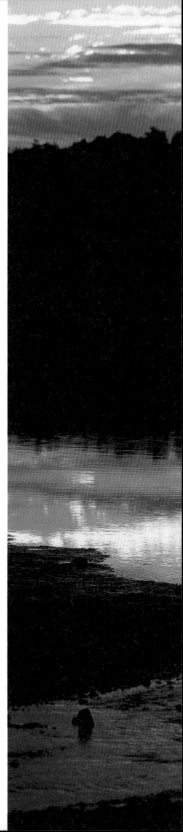

Worldly Desires

In Buddhism there are 108 worldly desires (*bonnō*), such as the desire for wealth, sex and power. At New Year in Japan, temple bells are rung 108 times to drive such desires away. Buddha himself battled with his desires, spending a long period in meditation before finally overcoming them and finding enlightenment. People who have vanquished all desire are said to be in a state of silence and tranquility (*jakujō*).

Bonnō

Kū

Emptiness

Kū denotes a state of nothingness, of being completely empty. The secret to finding one's Buddha nature lies in ridding oneself of one's ego, the source of all worldly desires. This is the opposite of what happens in today's affluent society, where people mistakenly think that satisfying their material desires will lead to spiritual satisfaction. *Kū* is about finding fulfillment in emptiness, rather as one feels completely relaxed when experiencing the simplicity of a Zen garden.

 Mu

Nothingness

Mu means nothingness. Because in nothingness there are no causes and no effects, no desires and no resulting worries, in there that enlightenment is to be found. The starting point for reaching *mu* is to look at things in a comparative and objective manner, rather than exclusively from one's own point of view. This attitude comes naturally to the Japanese with their focus on group harmony.

悟り Satori

Enlightenment

To attain *satori* ("enlightenment") a person must get rid of all their desires and enmities at the source.
Followers of some sects believe enlightenment can be achieved through chanting; others think the
way lies through self-discipline and meditation.

At the Hieizan, head temple of the Tendai sect, *satori* is achieved by hiking through the mountains
for between 30 and 80 kilometers a day for one thousand days. From the 700th day, the supplicant
must only read the sutras, foregoing eating, drinking, sleeping or sitting for seven-and-a-half days.

Relationships

En is a word for a relationship, from first meeting to farewell, and the bonds that it creates. The Japanese believe that good will come, either in this life or the next, to people who treat others well. The word *en* encompasses all the relationships a person has formed in this life or previous lives.

 En

Reincarnation

According to *rinne*, all living things follow the laws of the universe and the Buddha: they are born into this world in one form, die, and are then reborn in another form in an endless cycle. In present-day Japan, though not many people have a literal belief in reincarnation, many continue to believe (somewhat vaguely) that one's spirit lingers after death and remains near one's descendants, protecting them when necessary.

Rinne

Cause and Effect

Inga is often translated as "cause and effect." In a Buddhist context, the phrase *inga ōhō* means "as a man sows, so shall he reap." In other words, there is always prior cause for whatever pains or difficulties one is suffering now. A man who did not take proper care of his parents might be neglected by his children, a classic case of *inga ōhō*.

Inga

Muen

Without Ties

The recent phenomenon of old people dying alone after losing touch with family or friends has prompted much talk of *muenshi* ("death without ties") in Japan. Although the Japanese still value their ties to organizations or groups, the bonds of family are weakening. These days there is more emphasis on the nuclear family (husband, wife and children) than on the extended family.

Chapter
6

Build Trust

Trust (*shin*) refers to a strong,
stable bond established between people.

信 Shin

Trust

Shin refers to a strong, stable bond between people. The ideogram for *shin* consists of two components: "person" on the left and "speak" on the right. Trust is the result of what people say to one another, in particular the act of keeping the promises they make.

Jingi 仁義

Moral Code

The word *jingi* is composed of the characters for "benevolence" and "obligation." It denotes the importance of honoring one's commitments. *Jingi* is an especially important value for the yakuza. Even now many Japanese gangster movie revolve around complications resulting from the commitments between a yakuza boss and an underling.

Chapter

7

徳を養う

Develop Virtue

The principle of virtue (*toku*) teaches what is necessary to be wise.

Toku

Virtue

Toku means virtue. What constitutes virtue for the Japanese? It is a combination of modesty (*kenjō*), sensitivity to others' feelings (*jō*) and a proper sense of duty or obligation (*giri*). A virtuous person also enjoys life, even while observing the proper etiquette, and can adjust to any twists and turns in life's road.

Shame

Haji is not simply doing something embarrassing; it means doing something that stains one's good name and costs one one's honor. Westerners worry about sins. The Japanese worry about shame. *Haji* is not purely introspective. For example, a soldier who deserted his unit in battle would not only have to come to terms with himself for committing such a shameful act, he would also have to deal with the *haji* he had brought on his family and his comrades. With their concern to maintain harmony, the Japanese can be reluctant to do anything different from the group for fear this could result in *haji*.

Haji

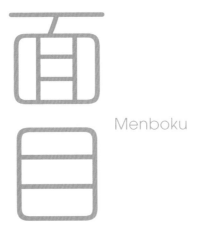

Menboku

Face

The Japanese, like the Chinese, have the concept of "face" (*menboku*) and are anxious not to lose face before other people. For example, if a person were to openly oppose his boss during a meeting, the boss would be placed in an embarrassing position and made to lose face. It is therefore better for the subordinate to seek a different place, or *ba*, to present his views in order to maintain group harmony.

Acceptance

Human beings stand below the gods in the great hierarchy. We cannot overcome death, see the future or change the past. There are clear limits to what we can do. *Teikan*, meaning "acceptance" or "resignation," refers to the wisdom of understanding human limitations and discovering one's role within those limitations.

Teikan

Understand Beauty

Among other things, the Japanese concept of beauty (*bi*)
cherishes the natural ebb and flow of the seasons.

Chapter

8

Wabi

Beauty in Simplicity

Wabi is the austere beauty found in simple, even stark, things. The concept emerged as part of the tea ceremony in the 15th century. Over time it moved beyond physical objects like simple tea implements to merge with Zen and become a life philosophy based on rejecting anything showy or wasteful. *Wabi* can also be enjoyed in observing the changing seasons while reflecting on the impermanence of things.

寂

Sabi

び

Beauty in Decay

Sabi is the beauty of things that are old and in a state of decay. For example, one might see *sabi* in the worn grain of the polished wood of the corridors in an old Japanese house; an old statue of the Buddha, the gold lacquer peeled off to reveal the bare wood beneath; or moss-covered rocks in the garden.

Tsuya

Refinement

During the Edo era there were contrasting concepts of what was refined (*tsuya*). On the one hand, the townspeople liked to dress up showily, copying the styles of the courtesans and dandies in the *ukiyoe* woodblock prints. On the other hand, regulations promoting frugality (plus the age-old influence of *wabi* and *sabi*) encouraged them to seek more subtle expressions of fashion and luxury. Metropolitan style thus consists in finding the perfect balance between the flashy and the austere.

Miyabi

Elegance

The emperor and his court were based in Kyoto for one thousand years. Over that time, the imperial court developed a unique culture of graceful elegance called *miyabi*. With the wars of the latter half of the 15th and early 16th centuries, the central government in Kyoto went into decline and power shifted to the regional lords, or *daimyō*. Ironically, this helped the culture of Kyoto spread throughout Japan. However, when the central government moved to Edo (now Tokyo) in the early 17th century, the culture of the townspeople flourished, while that of the nobles of Kyoto faded.

Chic

Iki, often translated as "chic," represents the dandyism of the Edo era. Often displays of *iki* are subtle but effective. Placing a single camellia in a vase in a room, for instance, to give visitors a sense of peace and to indicate the season would qualify as *iki*.

Iki is not just about matters of style. Imagine that an Edo-era man committed a robbery to buy medicine for his sick mother and the judge trying the case found him a job instead of punishing him. Here *iki* consists of someone in authority understanding the needs of the common man.

Iki

YŌ 妖

Bewitching

The word *yō* connotes a strange, otherworldly beauty. The word *yōen*, for example, describes the demon-like beauty of a woman seducing a man, while *yōkai* are the vengeful spirits of people who have been transformed after death into foxes and other animals.

For the Japanese beauty and death are often intertwined, whether in the pleasure derived from contemplating soon-to-die cherry blossoms or the samurai desire to die a beautiful death. *Yō* is the word that encapsulates this eerie, supernatural concept of beauty.

The Erotic

Iro, the ideogram for color, also means "love" or "sex." With the exception of the stern Confucian attitudes of the samurai class, the Japanese in general have tended to be very open-minded about sex. *Iro* is part and parcel of the drinking and nightlife culture of the big city. Kabuki and *bunraku* (puppet theater) plays about sex scandals and the erotic woodblock prints known as *shunga* are classic examples of *iro*-based culture. To this day, Japan remains remarkably unprudish. Many visitors to the country, accustomed to Christian sexual taboos, are amazed at the vigor and openness of Japan's "pleasure" industry.

Iro

Yūgen

Profound Tranquility

Yūgen are the subtle but profound emotions evoked by contemplating old, decaying or starkly simple things. *Yūgen* can also be found in the uneasy feelings caused by the encroaching darkness of evening or the sense of some vast power at work in the universe behind the subtlest changes of the seasons. *Yūgen* is an important part of the aesthetics of the Noh drama, especially in scenes where the dead speak of their trials.

Fūryū

Cultured

Fūryū refers to the capacity to enjoy beautiful things such as the sight of the full moon on a clear autumn night. A person who can properly savor such things is called *fūryūjin*, a person of culture. The ideograms for *fūryū* mean "flow with the wind," and a true *fūryūjin* can express his or her appreciation of traditional Japanese beauty in a seemingly effortless way, as naturally as the wind blows.

Profiles

photography
Katsuhiko Mizuno

Born in Kamigyō ward, Kyoto, in 1941, Katsuhiko Mizuno graduated in literature from Dōshisha University before continuing his studies in the postgraduate course of the Tokyo College of Photography, graduating in 1967. In 1969 he began photographing the scenery, gardens, architecture, and other aspects of Kyoto. In 2000 he repaired a Nishijin "townhouse" and opened a photographic studio free of charge to the public. He is a member of the Japan Professional Photographers Society and the Japan Society for Arts and History of Photography. He is the author of 120 books and photography collections.

photography
Hidehiko Mizuno

Born in Kyoto in 1968, Hidehiko Mizuno studied photography under his father-in-law Katsuhiko Mizuno. He became enthralled by Kyoto's beautiful scenery, its history, and the profundity of its culture, and began producing photographic work focused on Shinto shrines and Buddhist temples. Thereafter he continued to photograph the dignified face of Kyoto, the transition of its four seasons, and the mysterious profundity of its scenery. Today he is actively engaged in writing for photography magazines, acting as the official photographer for Kitano Tenmangū shrine, and taking part in radio programs, talks, lectures, and photography instruction.

text

Yoji Yamakuse

Born in Oita prefecture in 1955, Yoji Yamakuse worked for a major Japanese publishing company as its New York agent before becoming independent. In New York he set up as a media agent and established a consulting firm. Thereafter he attracted attention as a senior consultant at such firms as the Clark Consulting Group, dealing with cross-cultural businesses. He has been active as a consultant for nearly 100 Japanese and American global firms, focusing principally on personnel management and staff training. In particular, he has participated in the initiating and forwarding of joint projects in cross-cultural environments.

translation

Michael A. Cooney

Mr. Cooney first came to Japan in 1962 when his father's work required that the family relocate, and he has since resided in Japan for a total of more than 30 years. After spending many years in developing international markets, especially in Japan, China, and South East Asia, he is now focusing on writing about Japan and translation. He lives on the Shonan coast.

Description of Photograph

2

Thousand Torii gates,
Fushimi Inari shrine.

6

The character for
"great," a send-off fire.

8

Cherry blossoms
scattered on water.

10

Scattering of cherry
blossoms, Sagano.

15

Small "townhouse"
garden, Kyoto.

17

Inoue Residence,
Sagano.

19

Shimogamo shrine.

21

Hassōseki teahouse,
Konchiin temple.

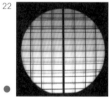

22

Ihōan teahouse,
Kōdaiji temple.

25

Kamigamo shrine.

27

Nishijin weaving.

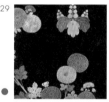

29

Design on back of
front door, mausoleum
of Lord Hideyoshi,
Kōdaiji temple.

31

Bamboo forest,
Nishiyama, Kyoto.

32

Katana, Japanese
sword.
© YUKIO TANAKA/SEBUN
PHOTO/amanaimages

34

Sōdō hall, Kenninji
temple.

36

Clogs of an itinerant
monk, Kenninji
temple.

38

Kūya Waterfall.

41

New Year's dishes, Kyoto.

43

Burning torches in Saga, Seiryōji temple.

45

Sunset in Nishiyama, Kyoto.

47

Going the rounds of New Year's greetings.

48

Washing yūzen in river, Kamogawa river.

51

Rakushisha cottage, Sagano.

53
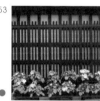
Morning glories and Itoya lattice, Kyoto.

55

Lantern floating, Arashiyama.

56

Rakushisha cottage, Sagano.

59

Thousand Torii gates, Fushimi Inari shrine.

60

Arrow Ceremony, Shimogamo shrine.

63

Misty morning sun, Okusaga.

64

Shimogamo shrine.

67

Autumn Hassaku Festival, Matsunoo shrine.

69

Seated image of Amida Buddha, Mimurotoji temple.

71 Memorial to Priest Hōnen, Hōnenin temple.

73 Sagano district.

74 Hirosawa Pond.

77 Nail (Pain) Removing Jizō, Shakuzōji temple.

78 Sagano district.

81 Moon over Sagano.

83 Daiōen garden, Hōjō, Kenninji temple.

85 Otaginenbutsuji temple.

87 The character for "great," a send-off fire.

89 Hōjōchi pond, Tenryūji temple.

90 Thousand Lantern Memorial Service, Adashinonenbutsuji temple.

95 Doll Floating Festival, Kamigamo shrine.

97 Oblong brazier, Kyoto.

99 View of snowy small garden through sliding screen, "townhouse", Kyoto.

101 Jōjakkōji temple.

103 Sliding screen next to alcove, "townhouse", Kyoto.

" April. "   love DOH.